Everyone I Love Immortal

Everyone I Love Immortal

Poems

Catherine Anderson

WOODLEY PRESS

Also by Catherine Anderson

In the Mother Tongue
The Work of Hands
Woman with a Gambling Mania

Copyright 2019

Library of Congress: 2018965327
ISBN: 978-0-9987003-5-9

Book Editor: Gary Lechliter
Author photo: Robert Cole
Cover design: Greg Field
Formatting: Pam LeRow
Cover art: "Love Letters," sculpture by Detroit artist Leon Dickey

Woodley Memorial Press

For Robert Cole

Table of Contents

3.

4.

When we love one another the most delicate truth

of that love is held in the spirit, but my body

is the record of those that I have loved.

—Anne Truitt, *Daybook: The Journal of An Artist*

1.

Between Two Lakes

The moon seen last night and the one
rising this evening signal a passage,

come through, go this way,
echo, echo.

A dream of two lakes,
the narrow isthmus

between them, an egret's slender
body, wings raised as it descends

to shore. Who wanders in such confusion
seeking rescue by resemblance?

And who am I in this dream,
rough lake water fathoms

below, the humid sky locking my eyes,
up close as tears?

Forest Elegy

Pine needles collect fog, mist drips to the forest floor.
Add sunlight and what rises becomes

the breath of the forest, its inhale, exhale.
From afar, a row of trees follows the breadth

of a lake, its span or measure.
Breath and breadth, so alike to my ear lost

to the woods. One a kind of freedom
from narrowness,

the other, an impulse to rest.
In one I hear the scope of compassion,

the other, the means to feel it.
Both words abstract and not. Both cohere

in the distance, like death and depth,
like myth, like mist.

Ember Days

Walking inward, into silence, a trace
of gasoline on her fingertips,

my mother wanders wrapped
in the coat my father bought her

the year they were married.
I watch her pass from light to shade—

the landscape of a northern city
where brand names of cars echo

like prayers against the void.
My Southern-born mother left

her '52 Ford by the side of the road
near a field of trees she had never

seen before. This is my dream
of her departure. She wears a coat

of leaves as she walks
through red-gold saplings

that flare up between wheels
and broken ingots, the field ablaze.

Blue Poem of the Father

Riding a bicycle under the trees,
my father a young man
who carved the air
he drifted through, the returned GI,
the city reporter biking
a washboard road,
jacket swung on the handle bars,
linden trees afloat
in the vibrant present.
Searching his eyes in a press photo
taken years before I knew him,
I try to find their color,
blue china or dim brook water,
their lights captured fireflies
in a Mason jar to salt
the dark.
Now dark filed in a metal cabinet—
the mind's embellished
alphabet recited backwards.
A dozen reporter's notebooks
are what I possess, the pages
fragrant with nicotine,
my father's words written
in blue hand, the letters shaped
like jagged dogtooth
only he could read.

The Speech Correctionist, 1951

Into this fold of history I watch
my mother enter, how she heard

a sparrow call *here*
over here

from a Southern schoolroom.
How she walked through,

crossing like a cloud
to enter a closet

where a child waited.
She wore a black and white

alphabet skirt that fanned out
as she sat on a stool,

the child on a stool, too, catching
the spirant flick of her tongue,

her light plosive breaths
spinning a pinwheel.

Coal-black hair and maple eyes,
she moved like

a tributary carving
her own bounds, young teacher

called by a child—little boy
who kept his pencil

in his pocket, little boy
whose stammered,

purse-lipped trills
circled his mouth like a sparrow.

Dancing Over a Field of Snow

The most flavorful Detroit-area mushrooms are found on stumps or under pine trees. In the Soviet Zone of Germany parcels containing more than eight ounces of coffee, cocoa or chocolate will be confiscated. No foodstuffs or medicines may be sent to Romania. Hungary no longer requires certificates of disinfection for used clothing. According to Armenian tradition, the pudding "anooshabour" dates back to Noah's Ark. What happens to the displaced person who brings old country skills and crafts?

During late August, early September and into November factory workers on the edge of Detroit spend hours after work looking for mushrooms to bring home to their wives. Appeals for Lithuanian freedom and a pledge to continue aid to the Polish government exiled in London marked nationality events yesterday. For instance, there is "zupa grsyhowa," a creamed mushroom soup served with white barley or noodles, but one of the tastiest is "pierogi," a mushroom and cabbage dumpling prepared in a crescent shape and eaten with cream or melted butter. He was smuggled into Finland and then into Sweden. His arrest by the Germans came in Berlin the day after the Germans invaded Russia. For some reason the farther east in Europe you go, the better the mushrooms, Wojsowski said. Zither playing may be an almost forgotten art in the United States.

It does no good to spend billions on foreign relations and then on the other hand pass a McCarran Act which tells all races except the Nordics they are undesirable. To the average American, mushrooms may be just something to eat with steak, but to the housewife of Polish descent they are almost as vital as salt and pepper. A concert of six Eastern Orthodox Church choirs will be presented at

9

3:30 p.m. next Sunday. By European tradition, bonfires are lit near chapels dedicated to St. John the Baptist, with all members of the parish bringing fuel for the fire.

When we hunt for mushrooms, we cook them on hot stones and eat them with potatoes roasted in the fire. For the first time in the United States, a course in the Polish short story will be taught. Bits of embers are brought home as good luck against fire, lightning and disease. According to legend, white pebbles covering the field of war are changed by a miracle into stones for the hungry enemy to break their teeth. Often pickled or fried mushrooms are eaten as a meat substitute. Seal them in a jar with a mixture of vinegar, sugar and spices. Thus pickled they stay good for a couple of years.

The word "sokol" means falcon, and to many Slav peoples, the symbol of freedom. *The Russians will strike first, leading to the liberation of the Iron Curtain areas or Russia will collapse internally, but this is less likely.* A favorite design is the "Snow Queen," an Estonian girl in native costume dancing over a field of snow.

Three Volleys in Tribute to the Horse Soldier

As the parade passes the Soldiers and Sailors monument, three widows of Civil War veterans will pause to place a wreath. Poppies will be laid at the graveside to honor the dead of all wars. Jewish veterans will be honored at Hebrew Memorial Park. The Latvian maroon-white-maroon banner will fly next Sunday from the City-County Building. *Some of the federal judges are reluctant to strike down laws relating to segregation because they feel indebted to the politicians who got them appointed.* Items for sale include handmade lace, linens, embroidery, etched silver from India, harem slippers from Arabia, African ritual masks and handmade toys from Yugoslavia. The Edison Post Lamplighters drill team drew cheers from the crowd when they appeared in their elaborate green uniforms and high green hats. Mr. Boyd, who took part in a Freedom Ride of white and Negro Episcopal clergymen last fall, spoke at the 99th anniversary of Abraham Lincoln's Emancipation Proclamation.

Lord, emancipate our love from self love. The collection will help to build a factory in Poland to make artificial limbs for victims of Nazi atrocities.

Lord, emancipate our minds, our emotions, from hate of each other. Lutnia's singers took part in a program with a group of Polish dancers, interspersing traditional Polish songs with dances such as the "Oberek" and the "Polonaise." The traveling past president of the Polish Century Club, S. Charles Nowak, has become a stamp collector's dream. One of Nowak's letters from South Viet Nam was nearly covered front and back with postage from the southeast Asian country.

Lord, emancipate our lips from carrying into another generation the lies we have told in this generation. During the Polar Bears convention at the Pick-Fort Shelby Hotel, the association of veterans who fought the Bolsheviks in northern Russian in World War II remembered their fallen comrades.

We must be prepared to go out on a limb when necessary to test barbershops or restaurants where they are segregated. Ukrainians in the old country think of the "trembita" as a long horn, like the ones blown by Swiss shepherds. Candles were lit and the traditional church bread, "prosphora," was cut by Bishop Damaskin. He explained that the bread is made in two portions symbolizing the divine and human nature of Christ. One of Leopold's major interests is to assist victims of Nazi persecution in pressing their claims for compensation against the German government. A 23-year-old woman, the daughter of a Detroit dentist, who now lives in the South, today pledged to have her baby in jail rather than "give up the fight against racial segregation."

It doesn't make any difference whether a Southern black baby is born in jail or not because the whole South is a jail. After working on a telegram to Mr. Kennedy, Detroit Cubans listened to Havana radio to see what reaction to the blockade emanated from Cuba. Detroit is the home of the country's only complete balalaika orchestra. The instrument has three catgut strings, with a system of the semi tone, the whole tone and the minor third on each string.

Lord, emancipate our hearts from scalding pain.

My Saint Joan

Waking too late on Sunday, my mother
sent me to church with the next-door

neighbor, saying, *please, take her.*
If not, my soul would scorch in hell,

charred like a marshmallow on a stick,
my fluent, singular soul.

A girl in saddle shoes waited in
the neighbor's gravel, the church

by the river's old part of town
that smelled like eggs.

Holy water touched to my forehead, shoulders
and heart, a girl's interior logic shaped

like the balsa-wood spine of a kite.
Ashes floated with voices and dust.

Not too late I realized I am a daughter
who burns like water.

I found my Saint Joan hidden in the lilacs,
her billowing fleur-de-lis,

her bronze skirt, her suit of armor,
and my soul a white bone caught in the throat.

Toast

Three Canadian quarters announce a gift from a ghost.
Navigating the waters of solitude can be disastrous
and require a television tuned to CBS, the channel my
grandmother watched every Sunday night, before the
ubiquity of porcelain crowns or recipes for natural dog
biscuits, the latter she would never, in all of her expansive
imagination, have imagined. She unclipped cloth earrings
and set them aside in a candy dish as her sighs crested
and broke. When she was young, my grandmother
traveled between Ontario and Detroit without papers
until she was caught with a roll of illegal ham wrapped
in a blanket like a baby. Some dreams are seamless,
swallowed whole as a glass of milk. Others sink and
crack into bits, or become a cornfield middle, with wide-
panned swatches and dropped horizon. I spend nights on
my grandmother's sofa until the end of summer when
my father arrives to drive me home. He can't stand up in
her tight kitchen built into the eaves, so we move a card
table to the living room for cube steak and Red Rose tea.
My grandmother makes toast by sticking a fork in a slice
of bread and floating it over a gas flame. The bread turns
a fine brown tinge I have never, in all the rooms of my
existence, been able to master.

Phaeton, At Rest

A spirit once driven by a slender
black horse lay collapsed

on the hay-strewn floor like an injured
dancer, wheels splayed under the chassis.

In the festival barn of a highway inn
my father bends like a circus bear

into my mother's curved hip, as music
rounds up and drops, a rhythm I follow

from my roost on the yellow bales.
Polonaise, oberek, mazurka—the body

in its dance loops back to its origin.
I am alive yet mortal like the phaeton,

my youth a *swift carriage of a dark night . . .*
rattling over roads that one can't see.

I watch my father take my mother the way
a man holds a woman, a circle

within a circle, their twined whorls,
their locked spheres that breathe, persist.

Inventing the Shadow, 1899

Illuminator of delicate foot bones
and dental caries, my father's machine flashes,
then disappears into the blur of folklore.

A switch sent crackling waves between
two wires, then *voila*! a spirit-print.
Found in the cellar, decades later: sheets

of skeletal arms and hands shelved in dust
like Freud's dreams of his own anxiety—
forgotten, then recalled—the dream

of leaving home naked,
or of teeth falling out like hail stones.
High on a shelf rests my father's invention,

a tango dance of round coils in a box
of black bakelite and red mahogany,
the grain polished so deep I could show you

the original forest growing within.
Get to know your shadow he would tell me
through ringlets of smoke.

None of us in the whole of our lives
will be seen for who we are.
Once, in an experiment to see what

could happen next, I tore up my shadow, then
pitched the little pieces out the window
just to watch them scatter,

lit like snow in moonlight,
my naked shadow—
hissing and swirling in the dry black.

Women Who Never Married

I was the floor lady those years we clipped
tobacco among the slathered

bricks and open lathing of the cigar factory
on the corner of Hastings and Forest.

What fell to the floor gave off
the scent of sage, the back dock loaded

with raw leaves stacked against
the noise of sirens and car honks

and clacking streetcars. Those half-cold,
half-warm dawns we rubbed

our stained hands together, my friends
and I, women from Poland who never

married or even thought about it,
our names memorized by thin spires

of a church on Detroit's east side.
For the record, I hung my feet unladylike

over the edge of the dock and poured coffee
from a thermos as dishwater fog rounded

the corner like a cat searching for a place
to lie down and bear her kittens.

Armenian Chant for the Dead

Yom Kippur began at sundown yesterday and will continue until sundown today. Two women truck drivers have combined their living quarters with their massive coast-to-coast tractor and trailer and have come up with accommodations as cozy as any motel. Ability to roller-skate may soon be a requirement for employment at the Detroit Main Library. So far three pages working in the reference rooms in the library's new wings have been equipped with skates to speed up delivery of books to readers. Rabbi M. Robert Syme appealed to each person in the congregation at Temple Israel to send their dollars to assist the rebuilding of the Sixteenth Street Baptist Church in Birmingham, Ala., where four children were killed recently. *We are technological giants, but morally we are still children—we have dragged the prejudices of the Stone Age into the satellite age.*

The Jewish Day of Atonement is the most sacred occasion in the Jewish calendar, marked with fasting, prayer and self-examination. The only other library in the country to use roller skates to speed books to the reader is Denver's. The truck drivers, Mrs. Clara Hicks and Mrs. Pat Armstrong of Los Angeles, passed through Detroit on their way back to the West Coast from New York. With them were Mrs. Hicks' two-year old daughter, April Dawn, and a French poodle puppy named Curly. If Zaki Mohamed Mostafa has his way, the United Arab Republic will be almost as modern as the United States when it comes to postal practices. Mostafa has been studying American methods, especially the systems and training used in Detroit for the past few days.

An ancient Armenian prayer for the dead was chanted last night for President Kennedy as 250 bowed their heads in the Latin Quarter. Detroit's main post office is unique for the extent of its automation. *I would say it is unique even in the whole world,* Mostafa said. The Library Technology Project, a professional group that tests materials for library use, suggested Detroit use a rink clamp skate with rubber and plastic composition wheels that would not mar the new vinyl asbestos floors. Percy Sarkisian, chairman of the dinner, said it would have been cancelled because of Mr. Kennedy's assassination, but there was no time to tell the guests. Words dating from 406 A.D. in the Armenian "Hokotz" prayer were recited by Fr. Sooren Papakhian, pastor of St. Sarkis Armenian Apostolic Church, Ford and Evergreen in Dearborn. Mrs. Armstrong said the four spend virtually all of their time traveling between Los Angeles and New York with loads of produce and frozen food. *We wanted to find a way to work together and at the same time keep April Dawn with us,* she said.

Whose Name Means "Stars" in Arabic

Go into any cemetery in Detroit and rub the marble surface of a monument with your hand. Monsignor Jasinski called the period between the two world wars in the United States *a black hour, with racism, nationalism and isolationism rampant.* Training workers was a problem in Europe shortly after World War II when skilled technical men were either dead or had left their home countries. Although the parade began in what many feared would turn into a blizzard, the weather eased by the time the Detroit Edison Company Calliope passed the reviewing stand. *McNamara*, he said, *is pushing American boys into Vietnam like he pushed dollars into the defunct Edsel.*

Marble is a living compound made from molecules of coral and other hardshell mollusks, formed the same way as chalk. A USO survey of American troops in Vietnam showed the men would like to receive letters from home, pictures of loved ones, local newspapers, magazines, ball point pens, writing paper, homemade cakes, candies and cookies. How to clean the marble outside the main Detroit Public Library was still debated today. Soccer is one of the few things that brings ethnic groups together without any feeling of animosity. He was playing in Toronto and came to Detroit to play with an all-star team against the Carpathian Kickers. The Kickers won. An exposition highlight is the new ultrasonic image conversion system called Ultra-Scan that permits the user "to see the sound." Lebanese dances are based on stories handed down generation to generation. They are all authentic and not the type seen in nightclubs. One of the troupe's leading dancers is Kawakab, whose name means "stars" in Arabic.

You are inviting trouble if you clean marble with an abrasive, but if it has to be done, do it with care and wide nozzles. Even chocolate bars are examined by X-ray before going to market. Candy makers search for bobby pins or anything else that people along the assembly line accidentally drop into the candy. Michigan is an unfavorable area for marble because of the presence of salt in the atmosphere. The Legion is asking residents to send packages to American troops in Vietnam and CARE packages for the troops to distribute personally to the Vietnamese. Swedish Prime Minister Tage Erlander today called for negotiations to end the war in Vietnam while visiting on a trade mission here.

Some marbles are hard and others are softer. Marbles vary in character and resistance. *As you get older the Bible means more to you*, he said. *Reading the Bible in Hebrew, you get the full thought, the complete idea.*

The Glass Artist

My mother baked a glass cake, caught
a blue lark to fill it.
My mother stitched ribbon

to a pair of sugar wings,
laid them on a plate
of clouds.

My mother was a dancer, a baker.
She lifted lace to a sky
etched by the tines

of a translucent fork.
We ate her cake and didn't stop.
We asked for more

and more she gave.
My mother's heart a ribbon
tied to a bird,

starlight crossing
an embedded dream
of glass.

Contraband from a City of Snow

On the wall, the painting of a rose
unfurled its petals—the watercolor
once sleeved with layers

of shirts and wrapped in brown paper
of the Soviet era—
contraband from a city of snow,

this gift for my parents spirited
out of Krakow,
its colors blended citrine

and butter against a blade of indigo.
The artist was the brother
of my father's friend,

a Polish resister who jumped
ship after the war, smuggled himself
across the waves.

As a child I watched that handsome
man backstroke the lake until
the pines turned black.

Their glasses clinked, and I heard
a male roar in the woods.
As a child, I thought the rose

on our wall was creation pushing
out the sky. Now death
my constant, my left hand.

Weight Attached by Strings to a Flock of Birds

The stones exhibited at the seminar resembled bears, birds, foxes and some looked like bison. *Odin is shown with one eye open and one closed, just as the Neanderthal men made many of their stone sculptures.* The forward part of the ship was gone shortly after the torpedo attack. He grabbed a life jacket and went overboard, making his way to a raft even though he couldn't swim. *Tell me what were their names? Did you have a friend on the good Reuben James?* So far sites in Germany and Denmark have yielded more than one thousand pieces of Neanderthal art. *Perhaps many of our legends date back much further than anyone can imagine.*

The Sons and Daughters of Malta will send at least seventy large boxes of clothing for Maltese orphans aboard the Greek Lines ship, Queen Anna Marie, sailing from New York. Twenty-five years ago several thousand Balts— Estonians, Lithuanians and Latvians—were deported to Siberia after the occupation of their countries by the Russians. A week after the deportation, the Nazis invaded the Soviet Union, but most of the Balts taken away in sealed box cars perished. Stamp collectors, because of their international contacts, were major victims. The sinking of the Reuben James has a slight parallel with the fighting in Vietnam—not everyone favored American actions then either. Paul Perkowski began the old craft of carving wooden toys when he retired from a lifetime in industry. One of his specialties is a paddle-like device with a heavy weight attached by strings to a flock of birds. When swung in a circular motion, the birds peck.

Another of Perkowski's favorites is a weather vane with figures on it. When the wind blows, little men saw wood or move about. At least seven Detroiters were on board the Reuben James when it was sunk; three of them perished. In a weather emergency, the first priority is a person trapped by a downed wire or an iron lung. Breaking reports are sent in pneumatic tubes to the overhead lines center on the sixth floor and teletypes provide additional information. *Tell me, what were their names? Did you have a friend on the good Reuben James?*

Detroit Pastoral
The Detroit Industry Murals

Almost forgotten in the sense you have to look up
to see it:
Diego Rivera's *Infant in the Bulb of a Plant*

with leaf-veined head
and thumbs touching ear and nose,
tender bulb with folded knees

round as a calabash.
Between north and south walls
of hot metal and fire,

the child sleeps
a fertile dream embraced
by a pale green sheath

of cells, the trace of plant roots
and curled fibers
like a skirt hem of genesis,

fish skeletons and shells in the fossil print,
east wall frescoed as prelude
to the great theme of Detroit industry

seen now as we head into our own industrial,
what we all save or ravage,
not one of us spared—

metal gleams in the grass,
evening streaks
of rose chemistry in the sky.

And aren't these frescoes painted in the same vein
as the teachers Rivera followed,
that pantheon

of infant-Christ-painters, each ascribing to the child
their own era's anxious view of the world?
On another north wall mural,

a child appears again,
centered as a crèche with three wise scientists,
a donkey and lambs,

the nurse (or the Blessed Mother?)
in clinical whites, the child's arm extended
for the *Vaccination*, administered

by whom?
Saint Joseph? The child's frog-like head
under a halo of curls, the face about to spill,

a portrait as familiar as the little boy
around the corner, the one
Isaiah describes: "when we see him,

there is no beauty that we should desire him."
I knew a place once, ordinary
and unbeautiful where at lunchtime

mothers spread out an oilcloth
in crayon-tinted greens
and reds a child

would recognize, the same colors
found on the mural
Michigan Fruits and Vegetables—

a title Diego Rivera must have dreamed up
high on his scaffold
painting starlight against gravel.

My Apology, Robert Hayden

If I could pull grace
like a kite on a string,
I'd recite poems
of yours I once
memorized, the ache
a banked fire
in my heart.

If I could remember,
I'd see Detroit streets
of my birth named
for presidents or
the cloudy legend
of pioneers—Jefferson,
St. Antoine, Beaubien,
built out of asphalt
and tin, cement
pounded from sand,
glass ground back
to powder.

I'd see the blue black
cold of fathers,
their pine cone bristle
at the mirror,
a child's wind
mourning by the door.

In the eye of a kite
hovering above yards
of fescue I'd see

the city's neon gleam,
its diastole
and systole, the cyclic
beat of its making.
And the willow
and elm—a house,
a street, how both
came together
as shelter and path,
if I could commit
to memory again,
Robert Hayden.

2.

A Woman on a Bus, Singing

She embarks from the years
of our nation's long reluctance,
the wide terrace of her brow
against the glass,
the half-moon curve of her mouth,
her upturned jacket collar, her scarf.

She is young enough to have a mother who worries.

I cannot find her name or who took this picture
of fifty years ago from Selma or Birmingham,
Little Rock, Detroit,

the list endless.
Like tongue or voice, a photograph moves
the spirit from its perch, the spirit

a small thing before it branches into clouds.

A young woman apart from others yet
turning toward them,
as if to say,
hear me stones, hear me people.

And a mother who cannot take her eyes off the radio.

What They Say of Us Later

Their time on earth an unending chain of heat.
With days massed like weeds between buildings.
With breath trapped in fields of melted grass.
And the heat a net above the grass.
With arachnids alive beyond the Anthropocene.
With forests grown within the cities.
And a thousand lies floating nomadic.
With the Great Lakes on their knees.
And warming water flowing to the lakes.
With evaporation all months of the year.
With the Word Incarnate wasted.
With walleye, sheepshead, perch, pike, small mouth bass.
With acid-scented water the rust in which they swim.
And men who fish on a concrete patch threading the river.
And the rivers unpolluted then polluted.
With polybrominated diphenyl ethers, mercury and iron.
With the black-oiled tern and the zebra mussel.
With Queen Anne's lace pressed in a book.
And the green Earth swathed in aerosols, wrapped in sulfates.
With the green Earth bathed in oil, gas, coal.
With the sky blotted from the wild.
And beauty anvilled of all its folds.

Festival of the August Moon

Ceremony closed, crazed dragon stilled
in a cloud of fish broth and smoke,

I heard a woman's voice ring the courtyard alley—
small operatic sharps slicing night from day,

glissandos lingering in the iron-lace windows.
Sweet durian and plums the vessels of Chinatown

contain—trampled orange peels and silver fish scales
fragile as poverty. At the Hudson Avenue gate

I watched a dazed ailanthus brushing the brickwork
and thought of those who would never leave—

backdoor kitchen, hollowed ash drum,
a woman who sings to the thick,

honeycombed streets of her youth:
What love do I still hold? What echo do I echo?

School by the Bay

A pitched roof catches lumens and salt.
I see it from a Red Line car

leaving the bay, the school a station
in the last century for gutting

haddock and cod
and a nameless fish that shed its rainbow

scales down the spiny stairs.
In my ear, the School for English still chants

its provenance: three fires, a hook
on a wall who spoke in proverbs, and one

truthful shard from that lost era
of AIDS: a small-boned mother of five, laid out

in white, family too frightened to appear.
Was I strong enough, was I brave?

I came as close as the times required, a beam
out of a cloud, then faded.

In the last fire we ran out to the avenue
with chalk on our hands.

The women who spoke Spanish and the women
who spoke Portuguese rescued

the curled poster of Frida Kahlo who loved
to fry tiny fish from Lake Pátzcuaro

where water floats a thin membrane between
our one life and the next,

her face a calm harbor, lit bars of amber
hitting window frames and doors.

That Word *Glazier*

All afternoon I watch the man who fits windows
lift clear sheets to the sun, glass
flaking translucent chips from his blade.
Through this glass I can see the sycamores in leaf.
I move through the house on my schedule
of cleaning and feeding an ancient cat
who can't see her food. Mid-ritual,
I meet him at the window threshold.
He tells me he came from a dry region
embroidered by volcanoes, tinted with rain.
His grandfather lost the right to irrigate land
the family had worked for decades, so he
headed north to join a roofing crew.
The day he started to fix windows,
he told his daughter: now I'm a *glazier*.
Do you know what she said, even then, in English?
Papi, that word *glazier* sounds so strange, like
the name of a Super Hero, someone who sees
through ice, grinds down the center
of the earth into the next world.
How do you teach such a child? he asks.
He trims and fits widows on the side
of my house till evening comes, then loads
his truck sideways with old glass on open racks.
Before driving off, he asks me another question:
Why did someone tell him don't yell for help
if you're ever locked alone inside a building,
but get down close to the door and whimper like
a little dog? The only way in this country to be rescued,
he was told. And I can't explain. I can't even try.

O Candid World

In a bath of photographic chemicals
a grave marker surfaced from the cemetery

of the former state institution for children,
not a name but digits and hyphens

like a barcode printed on the rough wood.
Blurred marks on a gray plane,

a patch of smoke in the anonymous field.
To prove this, let the facts be submitted

to a candid world: there were children
in that institution given milk laced

with radioactive isotopes to drink
as willing subjects, their lives

of lesser weight by some great scale
that rises and dips, their parents

told the milk was good.
The old masters were never wrong—

suffering takes place
while we stumble, looking elsewhere.

A boy falls from the sky.
Out of the milk whose very sound

speaks innocence,
we could have lifted him up like a delicate ship,

pinned the wet pages with clothespins
along darkroom walls to prove it.

The Crisis

By wing by wheel by night
a flux unflagging as

the waves a migrant child pulls
up to her chin.

And one could believe the gods enter
with them

carried mum on their shoulders.
Hermes, for instance,

messenger god of speed,
wing-curled shoes soft

on the carpet as he bears documents
stamped in red

then copied for the new arrivals,
faces pressed

on white bond,
everyone's eyes wide,

planetary,
each face a charcoal shade floated

from the copy machine
like a swimmer coming out of the water.

I reached earth naked and naked shall I leave
chants the Greek

as mortals blend with gods
without whom the work could not be done.

One could believe Giacometti's *Falling Man*
drops slender against

the void,
a displaced person from 1950—

At every moment men gather together
and separate, says the artist,

then draw near in an attempt
to join each other again.

His *The Chariot* balanced
by the single arrow

of a woman
in hammered bronze astride

like a circus queen,
wheels spinning her pharmacy cart,

The Chariot bearing—
O abundant goddess—

sulfa drugs and mercurochrome,
tuberculin vials

and a regimen of
isoniazid,

the refugee center's sharp walls blurred
as the earth turns a corner, the sun

swift in its rose drowning.
Voices blend, fade with others,

a few coughs in a shirtsleeve
as public health has taught.

Or one could believe Blake's midnight
angel watching from a tree

in front of the police station
where a woman has been taken

after wandering all night lost
in a lattice of streets

chased by a sound "like a bell,"
(her words in English),

and the case worker zigzagged toward her
in a delicate race to rescue,

the case worker not hearing the ringing herself
though she believes in bells, their power

to signal and gather.
A sound "like a bell?" she asks,

not knowing what the woman heard
yet trying to hear it.

We Keep Eating Yet Never Ask

"Capital and labor together produce the fruit of the land
. . .yet the men, women and children who are the flesh and blood
of this production often do not have enough to feed themselves."

From the eulogy for Rufino Contreras, farmworker killed in the
California Lettuce Strike, Feb. 10, 1979.

Their labor behind a curtain of light,
daughter after daughter

sinks to earth though wind fills
with seed, each daughter

a carrier of seeds, her flesh a soft polish.
July fields a clamorous choir,

a bother we want to forget.
How do we keep eating yet never

ask who will feed us?
Still these daughters don't believe in despair.

As summer months flatten and brown,
they turn away. They become themselves.

Elegy for the Materials

Asylum a state of mind that strikes before waking, as in:
I have no feeling in my fingers anymore. They have deserted me.

On the road they tried to guess the age of the moon, its surface
lofts and erosions, holes and clefts of deserted materials.

I was a cook for the army. She was the village seamstress.
The woman in the corner waits to speak but her eyes close.

Where is eternity? Are we falling? Dust, dirt, sand—
swirling particles jump before her eyes, unrelenting.

He talks about explosions they witnessed and missed.
To calm the listener, his voice becomes a soft, lambent room.

Leaves withered yet partially green out the window.
He carried water to a school in Kabul, the day lambent, still.

The asylum office overheated, his paperwork smeared by humidity.
On the wall a map of cavernous mountains to the far north.

Their child spins on a chair. *Fear—my closest, my longest
intimate, both of us locked in a country far removed.*

On the wall a map of the earth inked by small dots of humanity.
The woman, the mother, the wife, her eyes shut, lids fluttering.

As if the world opened its fist, scooped them up, and closed it.

Mirage

The road a bronze thread as Sister Jean of the Carmelites
drives like a teamster, head forward, hands gripping

the wheel while our friend Christopher, former Trappist
and confidante to acrobats and Houston hitmen,

names flowers and trees I can't believe he sees
in this swirl of green as we speed toward the stone prison

rising from the hills a distant sepia, buffed like an heirloom
photograph, prison name blazoned among the gentle

lady's slipper, the ailanthus, the wild hibiscus Christopher
calls out, weaving lines from Keats and a little Shelley,

the window open, roped clouds high above
and the city beyond the prison bent silver in the horizon

like a key thrown then landing sideways or *the mirage
of a space between nature and nurture*, a phrase that came

back to me as the title of a book read and forgotten, asking
questions we all should about chance and privilege though

who would know how to begin, I would confide to my
friends, the nun and ex-monk, as we drive along Route Two,

Sister Jean and Christopher, their wings aflutter like
Plato's bird mad for beauty only it perceives, their plans

for prayers at the prison gelling in their conversation,
though it's likely to be ninety degrees in the visitation room,

the guards' shoulders slack against the grated door as voices
begin to murmur, everyone seated on orange chairs,

flecked and round at the bottom, all seated for prayers
that become a soft choral as if to say, this is where we begin.

3.

You are Invited to Study the Heart

Freckled skin with a spray of moles
anchored by sterile cloths, the heart on view
in the cavernous thorax of the woman on the table.
Your white clothes donned, your instruments
laid out, this mark you make becomes your port
to a world beyond this world—knowledge you are given
because you asked for the correct line of incision
or a blade's depth, the heart's flow of blood
in the direction of its chambers when all questions
flood forth: how alive, she carried her heart as if you
would always find her, carried it as if it were
existence itself—a body so at home under trees
in the rain—four billion beats in a lifetime as if each one
could be counted, yet the attempt is made
with this heart chosen for study, knife angled to cut
the layered tissues, the numbered ribs, the vessels
finely channeled to reach the body's own still engine.

I Come Home Without Pictures

After the great circle from the west I made
following the swath of a Red-tailed hawk,
I asked you to forgive my swift judgment
of the blade-thin man who slid out of the booth
of the café where I stopped, tongues of tattoos
running down his neck and arms, or my sharp glance
at the order of meat afloat in the pond of gravy
left behind while feedlot trucks swung their loads
by the diesel pumps. I'd looked up from my book on the life
of Emily Dickinson to the sorry salad before me,
and heard a woman chattering at the tattooed man.
She said she couldn't finish her supper, wanted to take
it home for "dogs and cats to eat." Then she repeated,
"for dogs and cats to eat." Forgive my limited heart.
I wanted to ask why those dogs and cats didn't have names
and then remembered what you told me, how people
from the country don't name the feral beasts they find
but keep them fed all winter long with startling intimacy.
In the distance the Red-tailed hawk glided
on a thermal, its flight reflecting the terrain it scans,
the shadowed land beneath. I watched the man and woman
get in their car and drive off, a smoky miasma blending
into the poverty of stone. Home again I have nothing
to show you, the landscape impossible to catch by camera,
or an artist's hand, so better left to dreams, the long plains
poured out, low valleys a fugitive gold and two people
lost in it, a tabletop of fossil bones and dried-up sea,
the deep center of the country, souls passing souls—
an emptiness we all head toward—dots of cattle
and miniature oil rigs working their elbows.

Kansas Pastoral

I. The Egg Lady

To know the land so deeply you taste the flower of its pasture.
Every Saturday morning the egg lady rolled by, station wagon stuffed
with children whose platinum hair stood up like chick down.
My mother bought a dozen brown eggs from her.
My sister, who is older than me, says she has the same memory
of our mother rushing out to the road to buy eggs.
If there was fresh milk, my sister said, our mother bought
that too, because she liked the taste of clover in a glass of milk.

II. Birds of Kansas

I paid no attention to the couple at the Grill Stop Café until the woman lifted up a little girl and carried her out the door. In the parking lot, the couple swung the child to the sky, big smiles on their faces. A streak of pink cloth covered the child's head, tied in back like a biker's bandana. Her skin was translucent, cheeks a pair of faded apricots. Not one strand of hair was sticking out of that bandana. I thought she was about three-years-old and then in a flash I realized—my goodness, that little girl has just lost her hair to chemotherapy.

I am trained to observe such things. Nine months of the year I work in an office downtown assigned to the hardest luck cases you could imagine—teenagers with toddler children, ex-offenders lugging their drug convictions like a ball and chain and others with talent but bad health. I try to take care of everyone, finding low-cost dentures, pharmacy coupons or a new prosthesis. Because my eye is trained to note suffering, I make dark rulings: that man at the Grill Stop, too dominating, the woman too heavy, the man spitting tobacco, the woman smoking it. And at home, a cupboard full of sugar. If I were one of those birds native to the state of Kansas, my call would be "careful, careful."

In the summer I camp on the prairie, providing free help for anyone down in their luck. Sometimes I see what others can't in the usual give and take of life. I pitch a tent and hook up the camper wherever anyone will let me, usually an absent landowner with access to water and an untilled field to spare. It was late July when I stopped at the café, driving south through the Flint Hills, then a bit west, trying to beat a storm as I checked out a possible camp site for next summer. I didn't have a dog, since the last of my beloved terriers, Buster, had passed away in June. All my dogs were pint-sized rat terriers—loyal and fierce enemies of *ratus ratus*. I love a dog with a job to do.

People trust a sixty year-old gray-haired woman living in a camper, someone who doesn't know their mother, their old teachers or coaches. I don't care whether they attend church or have any money. Who they don't trust is a bureaucrat in a concrete maze from the jumpy center of town. I don't ask a lot of questions but accept the story the person gives me as we sit together under a blue awning on a summer night. I help them get the words out, then I hand their story right back to them. They're surprised by the gift, and I'm glad to give. At the end of August my time is up and I head back to the city, following the river like a cliff swallow.

When I was on the road with a dog, nothing used to scare me—8-axle truck drivers, Harley riders, serial killers with no headlights. But twice as I was driving through the hills I thought I saw that small child. The first time, the couple's battered Chevy was parked along the median, headed north. A dot of a pink bounced along the gray tarmac and I almost lost my breath. I kept wondering if they were in trouble yet I didn't stop. I drove right past them. I didn't have a dog.

My mother once rescued a grackle she'd hit with the lawnmower. She left the mower running, scooped the bloody bird into her gloves and ran to the garage. Shreds of grass whipped the air as the abandoned lawnmower vibrated under the apple tree. She made a bed from a garbage can lid spread with grass clippings and laid the bird on it, bleeding. This is where we come from, my mother and I: henhouses in fields of old tires and car parts. A dark-eyed junco at dusk, a sandpiper's marks in the shoulder dust. Cabbages and rhubarb under plates of glass. A red sunrise of oil and whiff of sulfur. In winter, stray animals circled our yard to be fed as my mother scattered bacon scraps and bread crusts.

I believe the wayward are an ark that moves through us—each life unique, delicate strands of hair on the back of the neck, aloft.

Later I saw the child again in my rear-view mirror, a flash of bright pink, arms and hands waving like bees' wings. She walked alone in the middle of the highway as if she were gliding across a lawn. I slowed down, held my breath as she toddled, hoping she would make it or that someone would grab her and scoot her back to safety. I felt as if I had been kicked below the ribs and spent a few moments deciding what to do. I'd made a life out of correcting the world, and there I was caught in the web of my own hesitation, car grill full of bugs. I was nothing but a failed bleeding heart. I glanced into the rear-view mirror, and the child was gone. I made a U-turn and searched as I headed south, but there was no Chevy parked on the median, no couple, no child, not even a skid mark. I drove a few more miles and kept looking. Nothing. The side-line winds I was trying to avoid had worked up and I saw a crow clinging to a branch as it bounced up and down. I pulled over to witness heaves of jagged lightning on the distant horizon. And then just as quickly, stillness. The front had passed over.

III. For an Egg

I find them up at dawn, father
and mother in the henhouse, counting
their eggs. They are the good candlers, passing
one to the other, each egg cupped in both hands.
O lovely shadow, O golden yoke of light
moving up a flat field, brittle

at the end of winter, brittle
as an ember. A field in winter my father
and mother's whole life, all time and buried light
cradled there, though long ago the counting
of eggs had stopped, their hands
still as snow. Who then is passing

through winter's arc now, passing
as corporeal as shards of buttons or peanut brittle?
Life's sharp and sticky edges, my hands
surprised by what lies inside a pocket seam. Father
carries a pencil by his ear, ready for counting
the odd hen who lights

from her nest, or the one who sits until light
ceases. Such patience, my parents! A passing
fancy, these hens, the neighbors judged, already counting
the end of eggs, their brittle
shells scattered, mother and father
ruined by the hand

dealt them, as if the proverbial bird in hand
had never been worth the two in the bush, so light-
weight a reckoning. My mother and father
never took such chatter seriously, passing
on their eggs, filling baskets with brittle
straw for safe-keeping, counting

themselves among the lucky. So the counting
began, carried off by a pair of hands
though the day was cold and brittle,
the sky, dull light.
The good candlers, so busy, passing
one egg to each, mother turning to father,

still counting in dawn's vapory light,
hands calloused as they pass
over the brittle fields, my mother and father.

IV. Oranges

In October my boyfriend and his mother would dress up
like Harlequins for the Renaissance Festival held on scrub land
shelved below the sky. Their collie Glen Laddie cowered under
the kitchen table when his mother donned her dangling cap,
waved her polished nails and smiled with two teeth blackened.
I was in my sixteenth year under heaven and knew who loved
me. We doodled during classes, copied rows and rows of
Cyrillic letters, fascinated by their inverted tilt. My boyfriend
was left-handed and liked to sketch through homeroom. Once,
when his notebook was snatched by the teacher, he penned an
upside-down dragon on his chinos, wrist cocked chimp-like,
inking his portrait from an angle. The bell rang and he got up
from his seat, the dragon rising in brilliant symmetry, never
to be repeated. He had short, spring-tight curls. Before our first
date he tried to straighten them, begging forgiveness for the smell
of ammonia that wafted behind him. In his family's basement
was a closet for Renaissance costumes and fringed kilts swathed
in plastic. The two of us shared a joint squeezed between the moth
balls and rolled-up Blackwatch tartans. The dog found us, twirling
his tail like a drum major. My boyfriend's tongue had just hit
the roof of my mouth when we heard his mother scream. We fell
back on the bags of kilts in mad, dance-like giggles. At home,
I played back our trysts, knitting furiously, propped up on my bed,
Diana Ross radioed in high staccato mode: purl, slip, slip, purl.
I knit him a four-foot teal scarf in a mixed basket-weave pattern.
Every night he wrapped my scarf against his naked chest.
A time to love and a time to weep. At the Renaissance Festival
years after we parted, I glimpsed him, then his mother. I saw
a string from heaven pulling our puppet heads and arms. I
watched mother and son, each wearing a black and white
mask, scatter through the crowd juggling oranges.

IV. Tornado on Hold

And here are my sister's girl and boy lolling on the carnation glider. I've brought them lemonade with froth on the top. At twelve years, my niece is almost the age when I began following my grandfather who showed me how to clean and trim horse hooves for shoeing. He would balance himself against the horse, shoulder to withers, deftly scraping debris from the delicate bottom of the foot. He worked with an unlit cigarette hanging off his lip until I struck a match to land the flame without burning his face.

At the blacksmith shop behind the house, he also taught me how to wait for the colored traverse of fire from red to orange to yellow, the forging heat that rises as you work the hammer and difficult to gauge in the sparking density of the shop. With practice, I mastered the torch and metal to form a perfect "U." Shortly after graduation from high school, I became the first woman farrier in the county, riding from farm to farm caring for the horses my grandfather had shoed as colts.

I tell you this so you understand who I am.

Yesterday one of my sister's steers felled by lightning lay dead in the ravine. We bound the steer's muddied legs with a rope, then tied the rope to the bumper of our truck. My sister jumped in the cab and pressed the accelerator as I guided her. I pulled and pulled until I thought my left arm would split from its socket, but we couldn't lift the dead weight of the animal. "God kill me," I said. My sister's children were there, watching. In the rising humidity I knew the steer would rot. I waded into the thick ravine toward the animal. I stood still for a minute to get my bearings, then cut the steer's jugular at the stump of its neck, sliced skin from flesh. Within four hours, I had butchered the whole steer as it lay in the ravine. Sweat dripped from my hairline to my hands, wetting the knife I held. My sister and her niece brought newspaper to wrap the meat in before they rushed it to the freezer. We were women with mouths to fill. When we stopped I saw the sun flash behind what I thought were swirls, folds—clouds the shape of viscera.

My niece with one tennis-shoed foot on the porch floor pushes the glider back and forth, like a cradle. My nephew, his body a lithe rope of nine-year old muscle, lies stomach-down on the cushions, almost asleep.

No tornado, no storm. Their father out of the picture, as my sister would say. I fan the children with a newspaper in the brief quietude on the porch. *Darkness hold me close, darkness take my arms.* The sky-blue ceiling of the back porch shifts to gray light. In a minute I'll get up and brown some beef. I once asked my grandfather if he thought I could've been created in the eyes of the Lord as part horse, part girl. He told me to always call a horse with a cadence in my voice—clear, low-pitched. You'll know the answer if the horse follows you, he said.

V. I Wanted the Eyes of a Child

After driving all day through the Kansas heat,
your daughter announced we would make
angels in the grass, an impossible
wonder—angels appear only in snow, don't they?
I fell back into the yard of Marion blue,
arms bearing down on scratchy stems, my legs
alternating like a pair of quick shears.
I got up not expecting a print,
and saw nothing to hint of an angel,
but your daughter did, tracing a pair
of green-gray wings in the grass.
For millennia, little bluestem and tall switch
grass have swayed over hills of chert, weaving
a subtle, almost imperceptible love. Tell me
if you know another name for it—
miles and miles of nothing before us, nothing behind.

Winter Aubade

If your face were not time-stilled, not
this photograph carried in my wallet,
but consciousness, a shadow

angled in the seat next to mine, you
could answer this query: Is the spirit
carbon or dust, water or stone?

I knew the risk to fly in January,
ice vapor hugging the ensemble below—
miniature pines and glacial fields, dense

patches blurred like cinder blocks.
We travel alone among others, each one
of us banished (we believe) from the republic

of Plato, we artists and time-wasters,
we slack dreamers watching the void.
And the clouds, ghosts passing by.

They have the history of sleep checked away.
Snow crystals bounce violet in the celestial spark.
A river touches a lake, as if two palms

brought together could carry it.
Water or stone? Carbon or dust?
Everyone I love remains immortal.

Questions I Need to Ask

Where are my blue gloves?
Are they curled beneath the cedar tree?
Are they floating on the Mississippi?
Do they miss being held?
Are my gloves jealous?
Are they bereft?
How far can my blue gloves be thrown?
Will they be stopped at the border?
Are blue gloves subtle or useful?
Do they send a signal to Saturn?
Do they cast light in a time of darkness?
Do my gloves remember their origin as the skin of a cow?
Will they struggle to pass through the eye of a needle?
Will my blue gloves love one another?
Will they be eaten?
Do gloves drop like leaves?
Or do they appear then disappear again, like the moon?

Conversation After Love

A bisque light still hovers.
We speak of our separate
grandparents, how they appeared
tapping the wall to find the switch,
folding softened sheets of the bed
they made for us—your ancestor,
my ancestor, their simple acts.
After love, before parting, our
breath released as one apparition,
our conjoined air accepting the transfer
of time and its diminishment,
we're spent, we're tired, we follow
any direction the conversation takes.
And those people from whom
we descend—ghosts riding
ghosts, alike but unknown
to each other, the plank road
they traveled or the wooden
turnstile passed through.
How we've held them in our minds
our whole lives: their pocket watch,
or handkerchief, the coal stove
they lit. One morning we woke
and saw them getting up
from what would be their last bed.

Winter Solstice

A good thing we did by the window,
my legs open, your mouth
pressed to the plum
scrim of my sex.
A proscenium of halogen light
poured as the wind threw knives
the quickest night of the year.
On our knees we did it.
For the walls bent to our noise
we cored the deep pink,
the blue edge,
a wheel turning against
the earth's last rotation.
A good thing we did.

The Lover in the Snow
Woodblock Print by Katsushika Hokusai

His umbrella about to close
or open as the lover turns
by the cedars at the gate
a moment before
or after, a fold
within the many folds
of Mt. Fuji not seen
in this ink portrait,
yet the great mountain's
immortality still a presence,
the lover's face bent
into his coat against the wind,
not seen but present in the mortal
branches weighted with snow.

Hologram

Colors walk into a room, take me
into their ethereal arms.
Love is my slow eye, an illusion.
When painting in oil, I learn to enter
dark first, the sketch a mere outline—
no pencil, no shading.
Dimension begins with color.
Blue, yellow, pink, the colors embrace
as shape and volume yet
my too-human eye still matches one object
to the other, a test of value. Color against color.
Wavering, laser light as if painted on air.
The hologram of the one I've lost come home.
I love what my eye sees. I love it.

Water Mirror

After Vicente Huidobro

All night, my mirror like a small rivulet
runs through the room,

my mirror deeper than the ends of the globe
where all swans drown.

A green pool surrounds the walls and I lie half
asleep with you, anchored in your nakedness.

Over the waves, under the sleeping skies
our dreams pass like ships.

On the stern I hear you singing and a secret rose
swells my love like a drunken nightingale.

Meditation in the Garden

Late spring peonies round the bush,
full clusters bent to the grass
until I think to gather

up the petals fallen from their heads in
chaos or love,
concentric curves with no open

lines as in nature all round things
circle back
to their point of origin—

flower head or handprint,
water drop or mouth,
loops and tubes

our bodies spin—blue capillaries
and light-bearing nerves,
the small complex heart

balled-up like a fist
opening, closing.
At my most melancholy

I remember
these spiral islands we are, spheres
through which

we suffer
and flower—even the mind,
silent guardian

poised on the rim
of thought, sweeps full circle
the garden it finds.

The Lake, Empty of Parents

1.
Laddered caps glide to shore, motors roil
the coast as green-carved water crests
and changes, but this is not their interest.
What they rally to in your absence: the golden
rope of Eros, infinite braid of no end,
no beginning—radiant, colossal,
a beast pulled from the Prussian deep.
How it breaches, how it sways, a topic
of summer-long fascination. And the names
they call it! One more clever than the last,
sonorous echoes of their own genius.
Hour on hour this toggle with the sun,
the depths. When do young men tire?
They think the lake will last forever.

2.
Or any moment you see them slip into trees,
skim the beryl blue ink of the lake
as they follow their nature, joined like sleeves
to one garment. A sun trace
behind clouds, a soft-lit day remembered
as the whole of childhood. They pile sand
with a red spade, heads tilted windward
they are mesmerized sailors, faces fanned
by a breeze that skips paper cups
down the thin beach.
A flock of gulls overhead interrupts
yet adds to the pattern, a separate niche
shaped by two sisters, glimpsed in their youth
before you vanished, another separate truth.

On Borges' "History of Angels"

Reading Borges in my mother's old volume,
I can imagine monsters, for they are contingent—
punk Lucifer thrust to the floor of hell,
minotaur dizzy above the wine-soaked Aegean
and dull, swollen Cyclops,
chimeras of our panic or angst
that vanish as light
touches water. Like the beast trapped
in Loch Ness, the face of Borges—craggy
and grey in Avedon's portrait, a face

I love for the extreme
of its particulars—vertical crease
and fallen eyelid, the photograph
as a framed homage that my mother,
for whatever reason, hung
in the kitchen—my mother both
monster and angel.

On the fourth day of creation,
the angels, fixed high in their firmament,
glimpsed the child earth,
barely more than a few wheatfields
and some orchards beside the waters.
While the beasts in our lives have faded,
Borges writes, the angels have never left us.

Night Window

On a path between night and morning,
I watch a small-town girl slip in,
the youngest of eight, hair cut jagged
at the ears by her brother O'Reilly as a joke—
so her half giggle in the photograph
by my door, her sister Marguerite's bored slouch,
brother Eugene's collar, cockeyed.
How she loved to dance
but wouldn't jig the Irish way, arms stiff
at the sides, eyes fixed
on a gabardine hat in the back row.
She tapped vaudeville in that cold town,
threw kisses to the parishioners
of Our Lady, Star of the Sea.
Drifting nights when I am afraid
of being alone the rest of my life, I conjure
the weird amber of her rented rooms, hours
spent wrapped in a sheet watching
furniture light up and fade
as cars passed through the black night.
All those brothers and sisters crowding
the room as if it were their own!
When I am alone, when I am a fool
at the very bottom of my loneliness, I invite
them back for another whirl
of dance and applause,
another spell cast to the walls.

Spoken Colors

I love obscurity,
what it means for truth,

how ink reversed
outlines an essence

and thus becomes visible.
Of all the spoken colors

the first one I wore—
my white confirmation dress

at the age of ten.
I say spoken because white

declares privilege, what you have
and don't admit.

The dress now layered in tissue
inside a rectangular

box, inert yet alive.
Light makes shadow

and dark resists, becomes truth itself.
Before knowledge I wore all white

into the crowd.
We thronged the church, girls

and boys walking the aisle as light
deflected, as light we couldn't see.

4.

Advice for Sleeping in Trees

. . .when to talk about trees implies silence
about so many horrors. – Bertolt Brecht

Note that trees are incandescent
as the memory of parents.

They embrace all souls, even
the willow wasp, yet you can curl

up in their branches as you
once nestled your primate nose

against your mother's clavicle.
Let no one think you a fool

for wanting this. Along the streets
of Philadelphia or Berlin,

the lindens in flower, piano keys
through sunlit leaves.

They are incarnate, they are holy,
they are seen as men, walking.

When a tree bends, unleash
your sorrow and sway into the arms

of Morpheus: Tell how your mother's
needle caught fire floating

on a skin of water, how the wind carved
a target in your father's heart.

Bleed

Who hasn't whispered inside that tight
room of the mind,

never will I bleed as that man there,
never will I suffer as others. . .

And I said the same thing,
I would never bleed as my brother

when nicked under the eye,
my corpuscular brother

whose blood throbs slowly, his body
like lead animated. Unable to speak

since childhood, he moves
with the pace of a man from another

century, someone older than perceived.
To spare him pain,

I would turn a ship.
Now he churns the drink, stares

with dark portholes deep as our mother's.
I am tugboat; I am dredges.

He waves and I wave back. What a lie, the empty sea—
we bleed and bleed.

Reading Room, Detroit Public Library

On the page a lake sturgeon appears, thin barbels
brushing the riverine, its primitive head
receptive as dark water conducts
waves conducting data only the fish sees.
No light needed for a lake sturgeon to feed.
The lake sturgeon swallows the body electric.
I don't think we're harmed touching it.

Whenever I read, the first person
singular arrives
with its lyric cry no one else hears.
My brother, born in the same cold-watered
land as the lake sturgeon,
never learned to think as an *I*,
to declare himself an *I* among other *I's*.
He resists by pairing each perception
with his own name, such as "Charlie's water!"
shouted when we pass a hill dropped to shore
and which means in my brother's idiosyncratic tongue,
"My beautiful lake, somewhere
I can't reach."

Lightning woven under water,
thunderbolts along a shoreline, how the ancients
met the lake sturgeon—pre-historic,
cartilaginous, covered
in bony plates. Of the lake sturgeon's vast multitudes
now diminished, the fathoms
don't suffocate as much as frighten.
The morning rains. Our books, our stillness,
an aqueous grey in reading room light.
When we were ancients, we rubbed
amber blocks to spark glints in the pooled dark.
"My beautiful lake,"
what my brother would say if he could say it.

The Boy Who Traveled to Feel what Shivering Meant
from the Brothers Grimm

Crepes and canaries, treble C and cumin, dust in your hair,
he swallowed the devil, he put the troll in a coin box.
What did he miss from school book pages of pigeons and train cars?
Said the father: "this lazy child will be a burden!"
When the alphabet serenaded, he fell asleep, the village
a smirk in the corner, the boy hopping fleas on a horse, a dream
unbridled as he fished-whipped the bedsheets.
What does shivering mean? A planet in retrograde, harm's memory,
or the reverse of warning? The boy went hither, he went yon.
His failures bugled, pumped in the streets as loud as collision.
A lazy burden, this child, said the village.
Not my life, said the boy. I am not them nor they me.
Hung upside down over hay bales and pasture tails,
the boy in a world skated by, a pleasure in the mind—
leave the devil who details his mother's
lacework, the devil spitting nails of human fear,
devil in the gravel, devil in the bushes. The boy who sought
shivering sought exit from their eyes, their ears,
their hungry, shrunken mouths.

Illusion

Weeks after my husband died, I traveled
All Hallows' Eve into the dark cyclone

of the city where I passed through the knotted
silk of traffic at rush hour.

Then I drifted along the avenue with a bramble
of sheeted ghosts and witches

until my friend—her face smiling,
mica-bright—waved me down as the last

coins of daylight dropped to earth.
In that quick shuffle, I marked

how the present envelops the past
like an accordion of mirrors,

my husband already twenty-five days
through his *bardo*, and still not there,

not home to the other side.
At the restaurant, the waiter, his head

and arms wrapped like a mummy,
took our order of bun with anchovy sauce,

leaned down to hear our voices through
the white gauze. I forgot it was Halloween,

assumed the young man was severely burned,

his injury a stillness held inside

as the room brimmed with sorrow, then
kindness, an illusion I kept to myself

as he carried water from table to table,
laid out the spring rolls with basil.

On A Hinge

My love flies out of the blue-grey cirrus to join
me in my car, dropping softly into the passenger seat,
lithe body turned this way, toward me. We pick up
our talk about the garden or neighbors from the last
time, our relationship a story I can tell my brother,
a man who has never spoken without help though
he listens to everything I say, tracing my words as if
they were beads gathered on a long string. My brother's
broad face beams when you first meet him as he extends
his hand in silence to start the rhythm of human connection.
He understands those blue flights into my car. He once
traveled by plane through a dark cumulonimbus, not
knowing as many of us ever know, where he would come out.
He was home on the ground when I asked him where
he'd been. "The moon," he answered. The moon
was softly buried, the earth cooled by last night's shadow,
the morning I looked down the driveway to see my love
again, his fisherman's knit sweater and tan khakis hung loose,
windblown. He came to help me fix the window high above
ground and hard to reach. An odd-working hinge kept
the frame in place and now the window was ajar,
flashes of sky reflected in the glass. He came because
I needed him, the house empty, unwieldy. He knew it
better than I and drew solutions to mind like nails
to a magnet. He was machine grace, he was imperfect,
without apology. I thought I could work the broken hinge
back together on my own, but there he was. He didn't look
at me or take me into his arms. I woke up wondering
what change had occurred between us. Another night
I saw a girl selling Asian pears, each separated by thin
paper, the sky combed velvet, awaiting a summer arc
of meteors, and the girl enveloped by household dust,
by faded stars. Mornings as I made coffee conversations
would come back, then surface throughout the day

when I did something automatic, like attach a file or
scan a document. The lit depth of the neighbor's bedroom
could be seen from our window so we covered it with
plastic that became a rippled, far-off herringbone.
I wondered as I often did, if being in love was impossible.
Near the door of my childhood home a bookcase
made of green bark grew from floor to ceiling
and served as a kind of wall against our chaos.
My parents, the gods, left saucers filled with ashes in the trees.
The acres of sleep I farmed, the months a constant season
of clouds, my love would bring me white peonies from the garden.
He had on the tweed jacket he wore hitchhiking from Montreal
to Vancouver. He turned and asked me how I was doing,
the sky a metal shelf casting grainy light with no shadows.
As Virgil writes, *we leave our sweet land, we go beyond our borders.*
The lake of my childhood is layered over nine-hundred acres.
Lake water laps the shore in constant waves, the rhythm not tidal,
as I once thought, but created by the shallows of the lake itself.
My brother speaks in echoes, echoes of what you tell him, as if he
were checking his own comprehension or playing out the sound
of your speech in his mind. The day I sit him down and tell him
my beloved is gone, will never come back, he repeats it over and over.

House at Cleveleys
for Neil's birthday

You heard lark songs on a marsh path,
the sea behind you, the clouds rainspent,

the house by the sea wall where you lived
the only house in a field of grass. Late evening

they led the baying cow to the room
beside the house, straw spread over the floor.

A lantern flickered. Too late for you and up
you went to your bed under the eaves,

your mother's kettle whistle
the last sound before sleep arrived

like a slender sloop. Through the night,
clouds opened to stars above the roof.

When morning came, what day
was this you tried to remember, voices

low as shadows calling,
come see the calf, come see the new calf.

Landscape with cliffs, these fragments

You wanted to see it again, my image
of that time: a landscape with cliffs,
the tide receded, the earth white at the end of day.
A path around Sussex met at the Seven Sisters.
I was with my husband's family, who
were my friends, the summer after his death,
and they guided me there to watch the sea.
People ran up and down the sands
in slow motion. Vacant cottages,
beach grass bent to the wind.
My mind had lengthened over the hours,
the crawl of jet lag, eaves-dropped
voices, harmonies. That morning my friends
had met me at the station then let me sleep
in a room full of seaside wicker where
a curtain lifted to an ordinary day
in England, gulls grazing the gutters,
the clatter of lime water in the pipes.
I had almost missed the Eastbourne train
at the uncoupling, cars merged as one long
streak of chalk in the dream I had lying
on the Indian-print bedspread.
Later we walked toward the circus near
my friends' home, past the promenade
and bandstand, the music full blast,
a woman singing, her eyes closed,
the large sweater she wore half-fallen
from one shoulder as she swayed
among the drinkers, the dancers.

April, Almost Spring

And what keeps me from speaking up is
I hear the counter argument

at the very moment my thoughts arrow forth.
Don't focus on the opposition,

my love once counseled the day I came home
and kicked the furniture.

No surprise it comes to this—all winter
the state has pondered whether to ax medical

funds for people who weigh too much.
At a final public hearing commissioners sit

with a look to beat us away like feral dogs.
Listening, I count the number of track

lights bouncing off one of their bald heads.
A woman asks a question and is told to ask

it again. On the balls of her feet she turns
counter-clockwise, a kind of bee-dance. How

humiliating. She rights herself, steps forward.
How brave. I am not sure why the sun

through layered leaves seems to move within us.
April, almost spring, gone for a complete year yet

his body full against mine. His face completely
green, his eyelashes like tendrils, his beard

curled upwards, tender head bent toward mine
as I rise to speak, my Green Man, my love.

Watching Ants

Sighting their slant hills
among the grasses I heard
your name called. You could
appear like that, your name
a soft phoneme.
If I feel the void
around the head, I shall
have won, says Giacometti.
Each grain of dirt rolled
between their mandibles,
the wounded carried home
on the backs of cinch-waisted
sisters, and the regimen
repeated, metal legs scissoring
rescue, the perfect machine
by which to survive.
But ants have no empathy,
and empathy completes
the logic of the world.
Yesterday was present time
when I heard your name—
silent, wingless—slow instar,
slow folded being.

Week of the Hyacinth Macaw

If this place were home, her own Brazil,
she'd nest in the hollow center

of a tree on the Pantanal, cobalt head swallowed
by the tree's noon umbra.

She flew to the zoo's tallest sycamore.
Among the leaves, the gold ring

of her eye offered one wink
then another. We tried to coax her down, a circle

of us gathered from Lions, from Chimps,
even the front gate. Nothing

would lure her— not filberts, not kiwi,
not the zookeeper's sweetest whistle folded

into the trees. I watch the shadows
under the sycamore, the arc of a leather

glove erasing the downwind draft like a wing.
One last long whistle and she's either home

or truly gone, flown from our hands like
a desire we'll never know again, dark wings

threaded through dark leaves, beautiful nothing
bird blended into the beautiful nothing world.

Above Fairyland Park, Where They Played

You'd never hear it—
notes scattered like mica stars, a tune for coal veins,
a tune for liquor.

Or see it—
heart kicked down a beveled street, past the rail yard,
the iron-colored water,

intuition packed in a man's billowed cheeks.
A horn so blue, so blown
to Hades.

You'd never play it—
blind whorl of his master thumbprint,
brass bow to the ladies—

Andy Kirk's Twelve Clouds of Joy,
Mary Lou's rippled ivories.
You'd never know

a sweet treble skirting the horizon,
souls descanted above the chilled tributary,
the crooked Little Blue.

Forest Elegy, II

Yet touch remains later, after
its disappearance, and I realize we are all a forest,
standing

or fallen, our hands palmate, the shape of a leaf
that turns the page
of our lives' angled timber. Come out of the leaves,

then—no two forests identical, the way each thumb
makes its own unique print.
I am not my brother's forest high up the mountain,

a northern slope
of beech and maples nor am I my neighbor's mountain side
of old oak and hickory, yet their seeds

rest within me. A tree the first pantomime
we make as children: elbows
apart, palm meeting palm.

The sadness of the forest is its floor,
all mineral substrate
and texture, the flow of rain and the floor's press

on plants, animals, humans.
Wind carves each forest face and its body,
a blend of climate, soil, fire, sunlight.

In the primeval wilderness, pines mix with oaks,
maples, hemlocks,
their bric-a-brac and crosshatched

elms and balsam firs.
Some grow side by side these brother trees,
others encircled by cedar.

I once read from an old book that a wanderer,
when lost in the forest, will stop
in his shoes and wait

for the pines to reveal themselves,
the upper branches whispering
as the air stirs,

leading him home.
I remember this, too:
every century and a half the Jack Pine

catches fire—scorched,
falling, seeds popped.
Like these pines, we vanish

then return: A coppice beneath the burnt
remains, a bouquet
of oak trunks branching upward.

Folded

How all through the *Timaeus*
Plato divides the soul: reason, spirit, desire.

And what of immortality?
Once I witnessed a blizzard at the peak

of autumn, land covered, fences down.
Under a crescent moon the herd appeared, black

and white as the hills and night.
I slipped through their luminous numbers,

the folded cumulus of their breath
the way a school girl learns

to cut serif loops with her skates.
All gratitude for childhood carried as the smallest

finger on the hand. All gratitude for the monk
who chiseled an alphabet light as bees.

I still ask, how does the soul survive its body?
On the page, a font resembles the word

it shapes. Set in *Legerdemain*, the type
is upright, not prone to regret.

I am no spirit but earth and ashes and flesh alone.
Now earth folded in sleep, now hills stitched in trees.

Notes

"Phaeton, At Rest": The italicized lines are from Henry James' *Portrait of a Lady*.

The prose poems "Dancing Over a Field of Snow," "Three Volleys for the Horse Soldier," "Whose Name Means 'Stars' in Arabic," "Weight Attached by Strings to a Flock of Birds," and "Armenian Chant for the Dead" are recreated from articles written in the years 1954-1967 for *The Detroit News* by James K. Anderson.

"My Apology, Robert Hayden" alludes to the poems "Those Winter Sundays" and "Frederick Douglass."

"What They Say of Us Later": Some images originated from the reporting of Jerry Dennis in *The Living Great Lakes*.

"The Crisis": The italicized line is from the Greek poet Palladas.

"Mirage": The italicized line is a title of a book by Evelyn Fox Keller.

"On Borges' 'History of Angels'": The italicized lines are from Borges' essay, "History of Angels."

"On a Hinge": The italicized line is from Virgil's "Eclogue I."

"Forest Elegy, II": The book referenced is Bruce Catton's *Michigan, A Bicentennial History*.

"Folded": the italicized line has been attributed to St. Mary of Egypt.

Acknowledgements

My deep gratitude for the keen eyes of Robert Cole, Maril Crabtree, Beth Horning, Gary Lechliter, Trish Reeves, Gayl Reinsch, Maryfrances Wagner and the Tuesday Poets of the Kansas City Writer's Place. I am grateful for the opportunity to work alongside the immigrants, refugees and caring partners who make up the community of Jewish Vocational Service-Kansas City.

I also thank the editors for selecting these poems for publication, some in a different form:

Blueline: "Winter Aubade."

bosque: "You Are Invited to Study the Heart."

Coal City Review, "Night Window," and forthcoming: "Ember Days."

Dunes Review: "Illusion."

Appeared in *Ekphrastic*: "The Glass Artist," based on the sculpture by Susan Taylor Glasgow titled "Happy Moment Number 27." Also appeared in an Exhibit of Ekphrastic Art, The Box Gallery, Kansas City, MO, 2018.

Heartland! Poetry of Love, Resistance and Solidarity (150 Kansas Poems Web site): "Conversation After Love."

Imagination & Place: "Festival of the August Moon," and "I Wanted the Eyes of a Child"

I-70 Review: "Between Two Lakes," "I Come Home Without Pictures," "Mirage," "Oranges," "Week of the Hyacinth Macaw," "Advice for Sleeping in Trees," "Bleed," "Reading Room: Detroit Public Library," "School by the Bay," and "Toast."

Southern Humanities Review, forthcoming (finalist for the Jake Adam York Auburn Witness Poetry Prize), "O Candid World."

The Laurel Review: "Dancing Over a Field of Snow," "Three Volleys for the Horse Soldier," "Whose Name Means 'Stars' in Arabic."

The Midwest Quarterly: "For an Egg."

Waters Deep: A Great Lakes Poetry Anthology (Split Rock Review), "What They Say of Us Later."

Zingara Poet (Web site): "Inventing the Shadow."

About the Author

Born in Detroit, the daughter of a school teacher and a newspaper reporter, Catherine Anderson was schooled in Kansas City, the University of Missouri and Syracuse University. She has published three other collections of poetry as well as numerous essays. Her work has been noted in *The Georgia Review*, *The Boston Globe, The Kansas City Star* and other journals. For years she lived in Boston where she edited a community newspaper centered on the lives of Asian Americans and worked as a staff writer for area nonprofits. She now lives in Kansas City where she trains new interpreters from the city's immigrant communities.

www.ingramcontent.com/pod-product-compliance
Lightning Source LLC
Chambersburg PA
CBHW020919090426

42736CB00008B/708